The Euro

Should Britain Join:
Yes or No?

Anthony Browne

ICON BOOKS

Published in the UK in 2001
by Icon Books Ltd., Grange Road,
Duxford, Cambridge CB2 4QF
E-mail: info@iconbooks.co.uk
www.iconbooks.co.uk

Sold in the UK, Europe, South Africa
and Asia by Faber and Faber Ltd.,
3 Queen Square, London WC1N 3AU
or their agents

Distributed in the UK, Europe,
South Africa and Asia by
Macmillan Distribution Ltd.,
Houndmills, Basingstoke RG21 6XS

ISBN 1 84046 271 X

Typesetting by Wayzgoose

Printed and bound in the UK by
Cox & Wyman Ltd., Reading

Contents

CONTENTS

Preface

It's as important a decision as it is difficult. We are being asked to make up our minds over whether or not we should get rid of the pound, and join Europe's new single currency, the euro. Twelve countries have joined, one's definitely said no, and Britain's sitting on the fence. That isn't a reflection of British indecisiveness, but of the little-appreciated fact that in many ways the decision is far more difficult – and far more balanced – for Britain than it is for other European countries.

For Britain, it will mean ditching what is probably the oldest continuous currency in the world – if not the most stable. In its 1,200-year history, the pound sterling has fallen in value from a pound of silver to about one hundredth that amount. The British have far more historical, cultural and political attachment to their currency than, say, the Irish have to the punt, which had only been established with the birth of the Republic (and uncoupled from sterling since 1979), or the Germans have to the Deutschmark, which was re-established after the Second World War.

The economic decision is also more finely balanced, with bigger arguments both for and against. As with all the other European countries, we have the potential benefits of joining a large, truly single market, and eliminating foreign exchange costs. But the British economy has converged far less with mainland Europe, and the pound has been notoriously volatile against its currencies. When the Danish electorate rejected the euro, the economics didn't play such a big part in the public debate, because it was far more straightforward. The Danish economy is completely in step with the German one, and their currency has been very closely tied to the Deutschmark for years.

In the case of Britain, the politics are also more difficult. In France and Germany, who have gone to war three times in 100 years, there is far greater consensus about the benefits of more integration in Europe. Britain, which has spent much of its history looking west across the Atlantic rather than east to Europe, is far more sceptical.

The decision is so finely balanced that it has split business, politics, the trade union movement and the City down the middle. Ferociously intelligent people who agree on most other issues can be bitterly opposed on this one.

But come a referendum, it's an issue on which we will have to make up our own minds. By laying out the arguments on both sides, this book aims to help readers decide where they stand, and be able to justify their position.

Introduction

When the euro was launched on 1 January 1999, it was the first time since the Roman Empire that Europe had a single currency. The second time round, it wasn't the result of invasion, but of years of negotiations, mutual agreement and signed treaties.

Eleven became one as the mighty Deutschmark, engine of the German economic miracle since the Second World War, ceased to exist as an independent currency. Overnight, but after years of preparation, the fickle French franc, the weakling lira, the guilder, the punt, the schilling, the markka, the peseta, and the escudo all lost their status as national currencies. Germany, France, Italy, Spain, Ireland, Portugal, Finland, Austria, the Netherlands, Belgium and Luxembourg all stepped together into monetary union. Two years later, Greece dumped the drachma and became the twelfth country to join.

Thousands of foreign exchange dealers in London, Frankfurt, Paris and Milan cleared their desks as the former currencies became mere subdivisions of the new euro and it was no longer possible to trade between them. These currencies no longer had any meaning in the wholesale money markets, and ceased to exist in the minds of the banks' computers. Their notes and coins would circulate for another three years, until finally phased out in 2002. The old currencies would retire to museums and the cupboards of coin collectors, replaced by the multicoloured notes and two-tone coins of the euro, adorned with pictures of Europe's architectural achievements. (The artist had originally based the pictures on real bridges and buildings, giving offence to those countries who felt left out. The pictures had to be redrawn, showing harmonised, non-specific architectural achievements rather than real ones.)

The unprecedented scale of the project has led to unprecedented logistics. The twelve countries joining the euro need 14.5 billion new banknotes, worth about £400 billion. They are minting 70 billion new coins, using 350,000 tonnes of metal. National mints – only geared up to replacing small numbers of old coins – had to start minting the euros four years before their introduction. The mints have only a fraction of the necessary storage space to stack them up, and too few trucks to transport them. Banks declared themselves unable to cope, and demanded the help of the army to store the coins on their bases, and transport them on the back of army trucks guarded by soldiers.

So vast was the amount of metal being used, that it affected the world's metal markets. Unlike most of Europe's old coins, the new ones won't contain nickel, after concern from the European parliament about allergic skin reactions. As a result, when the old coins are recycled, it will produce a 100,000-tonne surplus of the metal. When news leaked out that the world market would be flooded with the melted-down remains of Europe's old coinage, the world price of nickel fell more than 10 per cent.

But even these logistics are straightforward when compared to the economic and political consequences of the euro. Twelve European currencies have been merged into one, creating the world's second-largest single market with more than 300 million people.

The 'europhoric' claim that they have launched

onto the world a currency that could challenge the supremacy of the dollar and drag Europe out of twenty years of economic stagnation, turning it into an unrivalled economic superpower. Consumers, workers and businesses will all benefit as it leads to greater competitiveness, lower unemployment, lower prices, lower interest rates and higher living standards. Ending the inefficient and unnecessary division of Europe into different currency zones, it will promote prosperity, and by doing so, promote peace.

The 'eurosceptics' believe that the single currency will be a straitjacket on the European economy, destroying its flexibility and hampering its growth. They warn that it will result in a 'one size fits all' interest rate, leading to a return to boom and bust, higher unemployment and severe political tensions. It is the first step in the creation of a European superstate and the total loss of national sovereignty. Some detractors claim that it will be so damaging and divisive, it will lead not only to recession but to war.

Nor is it just politicians that are divided. Economists, businesspeople, financiers and the media are all involved in a titanic battle of ideas, trying to win the debate over whether the euro is a blessing or a curse.

In mainland Europe, they have made their decision, and the euro is now a fact of life. Now the British public will have to decide whether or not Britain should also join. It is not a decision we can all duck: we will at some point face putting a cross by the 'yes' box or the 'no' box in a referendum.

The creation of the euro was probably the most important financial event in the world in the later half of the 20th century. Whether or not to join the euro will probably be the most important economic decision Britain will have to make in the first half of the 21st century.

It is not an arid academic debate of significance only to politicians in Westminster and academics in ivory towers. If we join the euro, it will be impossible to avoid its impact. Everyone old enough to handle pocket money will have to get used to different notes and coins, with prices in euros and cents rather than pounds and pence. Those with bank accounts, saving funds and shares will have to get used to unfamiliar statements. When travelling on holiday to Spain, Italy, France, Austria or Greece, you will no longer have to start your trip at a bureau de change.

On a less visible level, Britain's interest rates will no longer be set in London, but in Frankfurt. Joining the euro could lead to permanently lower inflation, lower interest rates and lower mortgages, improve British competitiveness by giving us access to the world's largest trading block, create hundreds of thousands of new jobs, and once and for all catapult us into the economic and political premier league. Alternatively, joining the euro could ruin the British economy when it's at its most successful for decades, destroy hundreds of thousands of jobs by imposing inappropriate interest rates, force us to accept higher taxes dictated by Brussels, and mean a surrendering of sovereignty that will destroy our ability to control our own destiny.

Nor is staying out an easy, risk-free option for those who can't make up their minds. On the edge of, but not part of, a single currency that dwarfes it, Britain's businesses may no longer be able to compete on equal terms, our voice in Europe increasingly marginalised as we remain outside its big project, and we become an irrelevance to the US and Japan.

Alternatively, staying out could allow us to consolidate our economic advantages over European competitors struggling to cope with a flailing euro, making us an off-shore haven of flexibility and economic dynamism that is irresistible to foreign investors.

In one way or another, the euro will have a profound impact on inflation, trade, foreign investment, jobs, the level of mortgages, the nature of our sovereignty, and our national identity.

The Labour government has said that it has no constitutional objections to joining the single currency – it does not see concerns about surrendering sovereignty or losing a national symbol as sufficiently significant. Rather, it is a matter of economics: it will push for signing up when it decides that it is in the best financial interests of the country. To help find out whether this is the case, Chancellor Gordon Brown has devised five economic tests. When they all come out positive, he says, then it is time to sign up, and the government will put the proposal to the country.

1. Has our economy converged with that of Europe?

Could we live with European-level interest rates, and is our level of inflation similar? This test is necessary to make sure we don't crash-land the pound into the euro, but have a smooth joining-up. (This question is answered in sections 1.2, 1.3 and 1.4 in the main body of this book.)

2. Is there sufficient flexibility to deal with any problems?

When we join the euro, we lose the option of changing interest rates or devaluing our currency. So if we hit the buffers, do we have enough flexibility in other areas – such as tax and spending policy and the labour market – to kick-start the economy? (Answered in section 1.1.)

3. Would joining the euro promote investment?

Would it encourage, or discourage, companies from investing in Britain? (Answered in section 3.5.)

4. What impact will joining have on the City?

Will the financial services in the City lose out if we stay out, or lose out if we join up? Or does it make no difference? (Answered in question 3.4.)

5. Will joining the euro promote higher growth, stability and the creation of jobs?

This is the crunch question: will it make us richer? Would joining the euro be good for the economy and therefore good for the people of Britain? (Answered in sections 1.4, 1.5, 1.6, 1.7, 1.8, 1.9 and 3.3.)

The questions are important, but have caused widespread derision not just among Opposition politicians but also economists and economic commentators. They are so vague as to be meaningless. Many of the answers are impossible to quantify, to conclude either 'yes' or 'no', and so will be little aid in deciding when the time is right to join. Many economists see the five tests as an economic fig leaf, or an excuse not to make the decision when the public are so opposed to it. In early 2001, some of the most respected economic think tanks in Britain declared that the five tests had been met. Tony Blair responded that the government would decide within the first two years after the election whether or not the tests have been met. If they have, then they will hold a referendum.

How the single currency works

A country that wants to join the euro can only do so after its exchange rate has been stable against it for a prolonged period, either in the Exchange Rate Mechanism (ERM) or its successor, ERM II. It also has to meet other entry criteria, or 'convergence' criteria, laid down by the Maastricht Treaty: inflation and interest rates must have converged close to the euro average; the annual government budget deficit (i.e. how much more a government spends each year than it receives in taxes) must be less than 3 per cent of gross domestic product (GDP); and total national debt must be less than 60 per cent of GDP or moving towards it. (For a comparison of GDPs from different countries in the EU and elsewhere, see the Appendix.)

When currencies join the euro, their exchange rates are locked irrevocably together to six decimal figures. At that time, the national currency becomes a subdivision of the euro, just as a crown was a subdivision of the pound, or a kilo is 2.2 lbs. The old notes and coins are allowed to carry on circulating for a number of years, while companies and citizens gradually learn about the new currency. Shops are encouraged or required to show prices in both currencies. Bills, credit card transactions and bank statements all start appearing in euros.

Three years (for the original member countries) or one year (for Greece) after joining, the euro notes and coins are issued, and then a few weeks or months later, the notes and coins of the national currency are withdrawn from circulation. Each country can mint their own euro coins, allowing them to decorate one face of the coin with a national symbol. The one- and two-euro coins are two-tone, with silver and gold in them like the £2 coin. One euro is divided into 100 cents and every coin will be valid everywhere in 'Euroland'.

The notes come in 5, 10, 20, 50, 100, 200 and 500 euro denominations, and have the same designs – based on different styles of European architecture – in all member countries. Each country's notes are identical and completely interchangeable.

Interest rates for the euro are set by the European Central Bank, based in the Eurotowers building in Frankfurt. Once a month, the central bank of each member country – their equivalent of the Bank of England – sends a representative to Frankfurt for a meeting with the ECB's permanent Board, to decide whether interest rates should go up or down, or stay the same. They set interest rates bearing in mind the wider Euroland economy, not on the basis of individual national concerns.

Who is for joining, and who is against it?

Businesspeople, politicians and economists are as divided as the population at large on the euro – if not more so. Among the general electorate, there has been for a long time a majority against join-ing the euro – roughly twice as many are opposed to it as are for it. Surveys have suggested that readers of broadsheet newspapers and those with university degrees are slightly more likely to be in favour of joining the euro, while tabloid readers and those with less education are more likely to be opposed to it.

City economists are on the whole fairly sceptical about the euro, as is the top management of the Bank of England, including the Governor, Sir Eddie George. Academic economists are often slightly more in favour of joining.

Big businesses and trade unions are largely in favour – indeed, both the Confederation of British Industry (CBI) and the Trades Union Congress (TUC) are generally pro-euro. But both have been deeply riven by the issue. Some trade unions, such as the engineering union, the AEEU, are in favour of joining; while others, such as the public sector union, Unison, are set against it.

Among businesses, the position on the euro largely reflects self-interest. Large multinationals such as Unilever and Siemens, which produce and sell across Europe, are caused particular problems by currency fluctuations, and are generally very keen for Britain to join the euro. In contrast, most retailers – for example, Dixons and Next – are opposed. They will face all the costs of converting their tills and cash-handling operations, but will get few of the benefits. Only a few of them have operations outside Britain, so they are less troubled by the volatile pound. Sceptics argue that they also don't want the price transparency and cheaper goods that the euro will bring. Some retailers with more extensive operations in Europe, such as Marks and Spencer, are more favourably disposed to the new currency. The smaller the business, the less likely it is to do business with Europe, and the bigger the burden of converting to a new currency. As a result, the smaller the business, the more likely it is to be opposed to joining. While the CBI – representing big business – is pro-euro, the Federation of Small Businesses is bitterly opposed.

And the same division splits the political class. In both the Conservative Party and the Labour Party there are big factions both for and against. Many of the leading lights among the Conservatives are opposed to the euro, although some of the old 'big beasts' such as the former Chancellor Kenneth Clarke and former Deputy Prime Minister Michael Heseltine are in favour of joining. Many Labour Party luminaries look favourably on the euro, while a number of the party's more left-wing members are opposed. The Liberal Democrats are the only national party to be unequivocally in favour of joining the euro.

For:	Against:
Confederation of British Industry	Institute of Directors
British Chambers of Commerce	Federation of Small Businesses
Trades Union Congress	Unison
Amalgamated Electrical and Engineering Union	General, Municipal and Boilermakers Union
Kenneth Clarke	Dixons
Michael Heseltine	Next
Peter Mandelson	Sir Eddie George
Unilever	Lord Hanson
Smith Kline Beecham	Lady Thatcher
Ford	Lord Lamont
Nissan	Lord Owen
Toyota	The Conservative Party
The Liberal Democrat Party	British National Party
Scottish Nationalist Party	Business for Sterling
Britain in Europe	

Euro chronology

AD 286–301: Emperor Diocletian reforms Roman coinage, creating first European single currency.

AD 765: Effective launch of the pound sterling, when King Heaberth of Kent copies the monetary innovations of Emperor Charlemagne, and produces the first English pennies.

1124: All of the mint masters are found guilty of debasing the silver in the coinage with cheaper metals, and have their hands chopped off.

1489: Henry VII copies the Dutch fashion for large gold coins and mints the first ever pound coin, called the gold sovereign. After 700 years existing in notional form only, it is the first time the pound exists in solid form.

1960: Monarch's head put on banknotes for the first time ever, after the nationalisation of the Bank of England.

1970: Report by Pierre Werner, Prime Minister of Luxembourg, setting out a three-stage plan for establishing a Europe-wide single currency by 1980. Werner claims such a currency will end wars in Europe.

1971: Decimalisation of the pound, reducing the

number of pennies in it from 240 to 100.

1972: Paris summit sets 1980 as target date for monetary union. Plan is scuppered a year later by oil crisis.

1979: Exchange Rate Mechanism (ERM) set up to lock together currencies of EU countries.

1989: European Commission President Jacques Delors maps out three-stage process for economic and monetary union. Report accepted by European leaders.

1992: Maastricht Treaty signed, committing EU nations to joining the single currency by 1999 at the latest. The Danes reject the treaty in a referendum, while Britain negotiates an opt-out.

September 1992: Pound forced out of ERM on 'Black Wednesday', renamed 'White Wednesday' by eurosceptics.

August 1993: ERM suspended and then relaunched in looser form.

1997: Launch of single currency is postponed because too few countries meet the entry criteria.

May 1998: Heads of state give final go-ahead to eleven countries to join single currency.

1 January 1999: Single currency launched, with

every country in the EU joining except the UK, Denmark, Sweden and Greece (which was banned because it was too economically unfit).

December 1999: The euro sinks in value below the dollar.

September 2000: In a second referendum, the Danes say 'nej' to joining the euro. Central banks intervene to prop up the euro.

1 January 2001: Greece joins the euro, becoming the twelfth member state.

1 January 2002: Euro notes and coins to be introduced.

By 28 February 2002: All national notes and coins – francs, pesetas, etc. – to be withdrawn from circulation.

Euro glossary

Cent: One hundredth of a euro, sometimes called euro-cent to distinguish it from a US cent.

Convergence criteria: the economic conditions which a country must meet before being allowed to join the euro, namely: a stable exchange rate, similar inflation and interest rates, and low levels of government budget deficit and national debt.

Duisenberg, Wim: the chain-smoking, country-music loving, golf-playing Dutchman who is the first President of the European Central Bank.

Dual circulation: the use of both national currency and euro for two months during the changeover period.

ECB: the Frankfurt-based European Central Bank. Its governing council of seventeen members sets interest rates for the single currency.

Ecofin: the monthly meeting of Finance Ministers from all EU countries

Ecu: European Currency Unit, precursor of the euro. It was a basket of national currencies that eventually set the starting value of the euro, at 1 euro = 1 ecu.

E-day: the day on which euro notes and coins are introduced and replace national notes and coins (1 January 2002 for first-wave countries and Greece).

EMU: Economic and Monetary Union. This is what it's all about. The third and final stage of EMU was the launch of the single currency in 1999. That's the official version. Eurosceptics warn that a so-called 'economic union' will lead to Brussels dictating tax rates.

ERM: The Exchange Rate Mechanism, which tied European currencies together in the run-up to the launch of the single currency. Its aim was to reduce currency volatility and establish stable values for the national currencies. The pound sterling was famously kicked out.

Euro: the main unit of the single currency, broken down into 100 cents.

Euro-area: the official collective noun for the countries that have joined the euro, as used by the European Commission.

Euro-12: unofficial shorthand for the 12 countries which have joined the euro. It is also the unofficial meeting, usually before the Ecofin, of the ECB, the Commission and Finance Ministers from euro countries.

Eurocreep: a colloquial term for the infiltration of the euro into countries that haven't joined. Many British companies – particularly exporters – are having to work in euros because of market pressures. You can keep Britain out of the euro, but you can't keep the euro out of Britain.

Euroland: an unofficial collective noun for the countries that have joined the single currency.

Some eurosceptics particularly like this term because they think it makes the whole project sound ridiculous, like a harmonised form of Disneyland. Also called 'Eurozone'.

Europhoria: the feeling of elation that swept much of mainland Europe when the euro was launched on 1 January 1999 amid continent-wide taxpayer-funded celebrations.

Eurosceptic: someone who is sceptical about the benefits of the European Union, is opposed to further integration in Europe, or whose spine simply shivers at the thought of the pound joining the single currency.

Europhile: someone who finds positive things to say about the European Union, is in favour of further integration, or who believes joining the single currency will save Britain from itself.

HICP: The harmonised index of consumer prices, the official indicator for inflation in the euro-area (just as Retail Prices Index is the official indicator in the UK).

Maastricht Treaty: The treaty that set out the framework of the single currency, and gives it legal status.

Pre-Ins: the official Brussels term for those countries in the EU that haven't yet joined the single currency. That a country would wish to stay out permanently is apparently inconceivable.

Stability Pact: Short for the Growth and Stability Pact, which forces governments to pay massive fines if they live beyond their means and rack up too great a budget deficit. It was designed to prevent countries who join the euro from burdening it with huge debts.

1. What Does it Mean for the Economy?

Introduction

The single currency – the merging of national currencies – is most obviously an economic project. It directly affects our exchange rate and interest rate, and indirectly jobs, trade, investment and economic growth. This is why business groups such as the Confederation of British Industry (CBI) and employee's groups such as the Trades Union Congress (TUC) have such a vested interest in the issue. The primary opposition group to Britain joining the euro shows its origins in its title: Business for Sterling.

It is in the realm of economics that the intellectual battle for and against the euro is fought out most intensely in the UK. Since Britain's economic cycle has historically been out of phase with those in mainland Europe, and since our economy is very different, the economic issues are particularly thorny for us. In contrast, the economies of Belgium, the Netherlands and Austria were already so closely tied to that of Germany that the economic issues arising from uniting the currency as well were much less significant.

1.1 Do we really want the same interest rates as the rest of Europe?

NO:

The main danger of the euro is the 'one size fits all' interest rate, imposed across the continent from Ireland to Austria, Portugal to Finland. If our economy is ever out of step with Euroland, that interest rate will be wrong for us and we will return to boom and bust. For example, if Germany and France are booming while we are in recession, the high interest rates needed to stop them 'overheating' will deepen our economic plight.

Because the British economy is so out of step with those of mainland Europe, we will suffer particularly badly. This has already happened to Ireland. It overheated and ended up with rising inflation because it had to slash interest rates to German levels in the middle of its economic boom. Even the European Commission has admitted such problems exist. In March 2000, it said: 'Overheating is certainly not an issue in

Euroland as a whole, but it could become a concern in Ireland, the Netherlands, Spain, Portugal and Finland.'

Joining the euro may mean greater stability for our currency, but it will replace an unstable exchange rate with unstable interest rates. As the Labour Chancellor Gordon Brown said, the danger is of 'mistaking exchange rate stability for stability across the economy'.

YES:
The world's most successful economy – with about the same population as Euroland – has just one interest rate, set in Washington. In the US, they positively thrive with the same interest rate stretching from Hawaii to Florida, Alaska to Texas. When California is booming and Tennessee in recession, for example, they manage to cope with just one currency and one interest rate.

Britain can only have an independent interest rate if we also have a currency that is free to fluctuate up and down – and the volatility of the pound causes great economic problems. In the US there have been occasions when it would have been useful to have a different interest rate in, say, Texas, but the costs of a moving Texas/US exchange rate would have outweighed any benefits.

NO, BUT:
The US only thrives with one interest rate because in the US people move far more easily to look for work, and because they have huge financial transfers from rich areas to poor areas. When Tennessee is in recession, it doesn't suffer permanent high unemployment because huge numbers of workers will move to booming California in search of work. The different cultures and languages mean it is simply unrealistic to think unemployed Portuguese will move to Finland for work, or that people from Newcastle will move to Milan.

At the same time, the increased amounts of taxes paid in booming California are used to prop up ailing Tennessee through huge federal transfers. In Europe, there are very limited such transfers – the central European budget amounts to only 1.27 per cent of GDP, and half of that is spent on agriculture. If we suffer recession while Germany

is booming, we will be lumbered with high interest rates, with no financial lifeboat, and our
workers wouldn't be able to move to Germany to
find work because they don't speak German.

YES, BUT:
More labour mobility would definitely be an
advantage, but people in Europe don't even move
around within countries in search of work –
for example southern Italians rarely go to work
in North Italy – and we have learnt to cope with
the consequences through such things as regional
development funds. The government can always
fine-tune the economy by altering tax and
spending.

But in any case, this is hypothetical: it is unlikely
that the British economy will diverge much from
that of mainland Europe once we join the euro
(see 1.2).

1.2 Isn't our economy out of step with Europe?
YES:
There have been several occasions in the last thirty
years where Britain has been in recession when

Europe is booming, and vice versa. Our economy is out of step with that of mainland Europe partly because we have much closer ties to North America than they do. More than half our trade goes outside Euroland, and most of it is dollar based. We are the biggest foreign investor in the US, and the US invests twice as much in Britain as in the rest of the EU combined.

The Treasury's own figures suggest that over the last three economic cycles, the British economy has moved more closely in line with that of the US rather than Europe. Since the pound fell out of the exchange rate mechanism in 1992, sterling has remained relatively stable against the dollar, but it has been very volatile against European currencies.

In contrast, the European mainland countries do a higher proportion of trade with each other, and their economies are far more closely integrated. In general, their currencies and interest rates have been far more in step over the last twenty years.

NO:

Britain's economy – both in overall structure and in its business cycle – has converged with that of mainland Europe since the late 1990s. With the creation of the single market in 1992, the proportion of our trade with Europe has been growing. The UK and other European countries with high government budget deficits have managed to get them under control, so that all EU governments are now living within their means. The independence of the Bank of England has helped defeat our inflationary habit, and brought interest rates down towards European levels. Long-term interest rates are now very similar between the UK and Euroland.

Anderson Consulting reported in 1999 that: 'At a macro level, the UK is currently showing more signs of convergence with the other EU member states than at any time since the early 1970s.'

What is more, once we join the euro, we are very unlikely then to get out of step, because enhanced trade and investment will tie us even closer. Most of the booms and busts that have hit Britain but not the rest of Europe in the last thirty years have been the result of bad domestic policy (which we can hopefully avoid repeating), or the volatile pound (which will no longer exist). External shocks to the economy that we have no control over – like a sudden rise in oil price – now affect all countries in Europe in a similar way. There are very few economic shocks that affect only one country, unless they are self-imposed (such as the unification of Germany). For example, Britain is no longer an oil economy that is especially affected by the price of oil; Spain and Portugal have growing manufacturing and service industries and are no longer so dependent on agricultural markets.

1.3 Isn't our economy more sensitive to changes in interest rates?

YES:

British homeowners are more sensitive to changes in interest rates because we have more floating-rate mortgages, whereas on the continent most mortgages are fixed-rate. This means that any change in interest rates in Frankfurt will hit British homeowners and our economy far quicker than, for example, it hits Germany. While Frankfurt might set interest rates for stability in Euroland as a whole, it will mean a return to boom and bust for the UK.

NO:

Britain's dependence on floating mortgages is a result of its history of high and unstable inflation. With low and stable inflation returning over the last few years, more and more people are taking out fixed-rate mortgages. It is another area where the UK is converging with Europe.

1.4 Isn't the pound too volatile to lock into the euro?

YES:

The pound has been on a roller-coaster ride against other European currencies. It went from 3.32 German marks in 1989 to 2.22 marks six years later, and then back up to its previous level. With such volatility, it will be impossible to enter the euro at a rate that we know is sustainable in the long run. The danger is that we may enter at far too high a rate, locking in the strength of the pound, and making our exporters permanently uncompetitive.

The dangers of getting the wrong rate were shown when we entered the Exchange Rate Mechanism (ERM) at too high a level. It was just unsustainable, requiring such high interest rates that 100,000 companies went out of business in two years and unemployment doubled. It got so desperate that the Chancellor at the time, Norman Lamont, was forced to impose repeated emergency interest rate rises until he finally accepted the inevitable and let the pound fall out of the system in 1992.

All the European currencies that eventually locked themselves into the euro had proved for many years that they were stable against each other. With the pound we have failed to show that, and to lock ourselves in would be a repeat of the ERM disaster, but with no way out.

NO:

Before Britain enters the euro, we have to demonstrate that the exchange rate is stable, and make sure it is at a level that can be sustained. Indeed, stability against the euro is one of the preconditions of entry set out in the Maastricht Treaty.

After deciding that we want to join, the government would then have to actively pursue a policy of currency stability in the run-up to actually entering. It would have to decide at what exchange rate we should join, agree it with other Euroland members, and then set interest rates to ensure that we stick to that exchange rate. It is perfectly economically possible – it is just a question of political will.

1.5 Will joining solve the problem of the volatile pound?
YES:
Obviously if we joined the euro, we would have the same currency as our main trading partners in Euroland, and the problem of a pound that bounces up and down would be ended at a stroke. This would help create certainty for exporters and importers who have been ravaged by the unpredictability of our currency.

Britain is very vulnerable to these currency movements because we are a medium-sized economy which is heavily dependent on imports and exports. The US, and Euroland as a whole, are vast economies with proportionately little dependence on external trade, so they can afford to neglect their exchange rates.

NO:
Half of our trade and two-thirds of our investment is with the rest of the world outside the twelve countries of Euroland. Most of our exports are traded in dollars and this is why the pound has been relatively stable against the dollar. However, the euro has been very volatile against the dollar, so locking the pound to the euro would actually mean *more* currency instability for the majority of our exporters, not less.

In any case, a floating exchange rate is one of the economic safety valves (along with public spending and interest rates) that can protect the economy from external shocks, and help it adjust in the global market place. Having a floating exchange rate allows us to compensate for differences in inflation and productivity between nations, and can help boost our economy if we end up in recession. By devaluing the pound after dropping out of the exchange rate mechanism, exporters got a big boost and the economy improved rapidly.

If a volatile exchange rate were such a big problem, there are plenty of other things that the Treasury or the Bank of England could do – such as set an exchange rate target – without actually giving up our currency altogether.

YES, BUT:
The EU is Britain's most important market. Britain sends 58 per cent of its export goods to the fourteen other countries of the EU, and only 15 per cent to the US. Since far more of our trade is with EU rather than the US, currency stability with Euroland is far more important than it is against the dollar.

If we don't join, the problem we have with a volatile currency will only get worse. As the electronic revolution gathers pace, vast sums of money are washing ever more rapidly around the world, dwarfing national economies. More than $1,000 billion in different currencies goes through the foreign exchange markets every day – about the same as Britain's entire annual economic output. These money flows can alter exchange rates very rapidly.

If we remain outside the euro, the pound will remain torn between the euro and the dollar, strongly connected to both but not protected by either. The pound would be torn apart like a child trying to hold on to both its parents who are walking around in different directions regardless. Financier George Soros – whose speculation forced the pound out of the Exchange Rate Mechanism – said: 'I think that sterling will be in a very dangerous position because it would be caught between two very large currency zones.'

1.6 Will the euro push up inflation?
YES:

In recent years, the independent Bank of England has proved very successful at controlling inflation. Britain is no longer the high inflation capital of Europe, but has inflation at a similarly low level to Germany and France.

However, if we join the euro we will be forced to have European interest rates which have generally been much lower than British ones, inevitably leading to an inflationary boom. The Governor of the Bank of England, Sir Eddie George, has said that if we had joined the euro at the start, it would be difficult to see how we could have kept inflation to the official target of 2.5 per cent.

NO:
There will be long-term downward forces on prices that are far more powerful than the effect of low interest rates. More trade and stronger competition will keep prices in check. The accountants KPMG reported that within a year of its launch, 40 per cent of Euroland firms had cut prices because of the single currency.

One of the most important influences will be 'price transparency'. With goods in the same currency here as in the rest of Euroland, it will be far easier to directly compare prices without having to convert currencies or incur any foreign exchange costs. When shoppers in 'Rip-off Britain' can so easily see they are being charged more, they will become far more demanding in getting the same low prices as mainland Europe.

What happened with car prices – where lower prices in Europe eventually forced British dealers to cut their prices – would have happened far earlier if there had been greater price transparency.

High levels of competition, price transparency and increased trade will force expensive companies to bring prices down to the lowest level. The KPMG study showed that 74 per cent of companies with variable prices across Europe thought the gap would have to narrow as a result of the euro. With Britain having generally higher prices than the rest of Europe, it can only win.

YES, BUT:

People only do a tiny proportion of their shopping in Europe. It's all very well in the Netherlands or Belgium where you can pop over the border. But British people are not going to start buying all their jeans in Milan and bread in Paris, and vodka in Finland. The effect will be marginal at best – perhaps it will only make a difference in really big ticket items like cars, and that's happened already without the euro.

NO, BUT:

Internet shopping will make price transparency far more obvious, with people being able to compare prices across the continent and buy things at the click of a mouse. The Internet effect will be powerful in business, where companies can search out and buy from the cheapest suppliers. This is already greatly reducing the costs of production, and these savings will ultimately be passed on to consumers.

Getting rid of foreign exchange costs will boost trade, making it easier for cheaper goods from Europe to undercut higher cost British goods. Furthermore, the creation of an enormous single market the size of the US will lead to economies of scale in production that will bring prices down still further.

YES, BUT:

The reduction in prices because of the Internet will happen anyway, for both businesses and consumers. People in Britain already buy goods from the US via the Internet, and just charge it to their credit cards. Language is a far bigger barrier than foreign exchange costs, so joining the euro will make little difference to this.

1.7 Will joining the euro boost trade?
YES:

By joining the euro we will be joining the largest single market in the world outside the US. It will enable businesses to sell more widely, achieving greater economies of scale. It will also enable families and businesses to buy from a wider, and so cheaper, range of suppliers. Both of these will boost trade and increase our prosperity. One study showed that, other things being equal, a country conducts three times as much trade with another that shares a common currency, than with one where it has to change currency.

Having a stable exchange rate with our biggest trading partner – Euroland – will eliminate uncertainties and so boost trade further.

NO:

We have been part of the European single market since 1992, when most trade barriers were abolished. Having the same currency will make little extra difference. Businesses can already buy from suppliers in different countries, and foreign exchange costs are marginal (see 3.2).

At the moment, we have access to the market while avoiding the disadvantages – such as inappropriate interest rates – of being part of it. The biggest disruption to our trade would be the return to boom and bust that locking ourselves to the euro would involve.

Half our trade is with the world outside Euroland, and that will get no benefit from joining the euro. All our trade that is priced in dollars will suffer as we lock ourselves to a currency – the euro – that is so volatile against the dollar (see 1.5).

YES, BUT:
Getting rid of ordinary trade barriers, as we did in 1992, is not enough to ensure a single market. According to the European Commission, prices vary by up to 16 per cent between the cheapest and most expensive places in the EU, but by only 11 per cent in the US. This shows that the market isn't working as efficiently as it is in the US.

Separate currencies also act as a barrier to trade, partly because of the cost and trouble of converting currencies, but also because uncertainty about the rates of exchange can damage profits. Only by having a single currency can producers in Britain be confident of what their profits will be.

For example, Canada shares language, culture and free trade with the US. But because it has a separate currency, Canadian provinces do around 20 times more trade with each other than they do with US states that are the same distance away. This is one reason why Canadians are on average 20 per cent poorer than Americans.

1.8 Will jobs be lost if we stay out?
YES:

Staying out will lead to the loss of thousands of jobs as foreign investors stay away and British businesses become relatively uncompetitive compared to their Euroland rivals. Without access to the single currency zone, foreign investors who are here will move out, closing factories and businesses; new ones will set up in Euroland in preference to the UK (see 3.5).

The huge economies of scale of the vast single market of Euroland will enable investors to produce more goods at lower prices, undercutting British companies at home and abroad. As British companies lose out, so will their workers.

NO:
Joining the euro would damage the British economy with 'one size fits all' interest rates, and so destroy jobs. It is being part of the European Union single market rather than the euro that ensures trade and employment.

The evidence speaks for itself: Britain's unemployment carried on falling, and foreign investment rose to record levels after the launch of the euro. In the 1990s, Britain created more jobs than all the other Euroland countries put together. In 2000, unemployment in Euroland averaged about 10 per cent, compared to under 6 per cent in the UK.

Past experience has already shown us that locking ourselves into inappropriate interest rates and exchange rates destroys jobs. After we joined the Exchange Rate Mechanism, 100,000 businesses went bankrupt and unemployment doubled before we were finally forced out in 1992.

YES, BUT:

The problem is simply that we joined the Exchange Rate Mechanism at far too high an exchange rate, making our exporters very expensive and forcing us to hike up interest rates in order to stay in. We have to make sure we join the euro at a sustainable exchange rate, so that such problems don't happen again.

Unemployment is not high everywhere in Euroland. Some countries, such as Austria, Ireland and the Netherlands had an average unemployment rate of just 4 per cent in 2000.

In those Euroland countries where unemployment is a lot higher – such as Germany and France – it has nothing to do with the euro and everything to do with all the rules and regulations they have that encumber their businesses. Unemployment was higher in Europe before any countries had even decided to join the euro, and since the launch of the euro, unemployment has come down as the Euroland economy has picked up.

1.9 Isn't the British economy doing fine on its own, and won't it thrive outside?

YES:

It is the world's fourth-largest economy, in the best condition it has been in for generations. Britain's flexible labour market and low taxation helped push unemployment and inflation to the lowest level for a quarter of a century. After the boom and bust of the 1970s, 80s and 90s, we at last have long-term economic stability. Joining the euro will be a profound shock to the economy that will threaten all we have achieved.

As a low-tax, flexible economy off the coast of mainland Europe, we are proving increasingly attractive to foreign investors. Staying out will give us the best of both worlds: we are in the single market, but outside the euro.

NO:

Britain was doing very well before the creation of the euro, but the world has moved on. The single currency – and the world's second-largest single market – is now a fact of life, it's on our doorstep, and we're not part of it. We may be the world's fourth-largest economy, but we are now being dwarfed by a neighbour that is rapidly reorganising itself and becoming more competitive. The ground rules have changed.

The impact of our exclusion was muted in the first couple of years by the Labour government's hints that we would join soon, encouraging foreign investors to hold firm.

But the disadvantages of staying out – shunned by foreign investors and undercut by more efficient European competitors – will become increasingly clear. By the time these are obvious even to eurosceptics, we will have squandered our fine economic achievements. Not joining the euro is the biggest threat to our continued prosperity.

2. What Does it Mean Politically?

Introduction

Although the single currency is most obviously an economic project, the political issues have proved particularly persuasive in public debate. This is hardly surprising since for centuries the national currency has been such a potent symbol of the nation state. There is widespread concern that giving up our own currency will mean surrendering our sovereignty and the ability to determine our own future as we see fit. Doesn't a single currency inevitably lead to a single European superstate? What would joining the euro do to Britain's international influence? Nothing better represents these concerns than the question that the tabloids have often asked: what will it do to the Queen's head on our notes?

These emotive issues are likely to be far more influential in a referendum than the relatively dry and arcane arguments about economics, as the Danish government, business and media found out to their cost. They combined forces to argue for joining the euro on largely economic grounds, only to have the public reject it in a referendum for largely political and cultural reasons.

2.1 Will the government lose control over our interest rates if we join?

YES:

Interest rates will no longer be set in London by the Bank of England, but in Frankfurt by the European Central Bank (ECB). When the Bank of England's Monetary Policy Committee meet once a month to set rates, all they consider is what is best for the UK. In contrast, the ECB committee is made up of non-elected foreign central bankers who will easily outvote the one British representative. They are appointed by foreign governments and, once appointed, are politically unaccountable. When they discuss whether to raise or cut interest rates, they are meant to consider what is happening in the wider European economy – in particular Germany, the largest Euroland economy – with just a glance at Britain's needs. The fact that the European Central Bank and its huge staff of economists are based in Germany cannot but help bias them to what is happening there on the ground.

Nor were the different national representatives on the European Central Bank's rate-setting committee really able to think objectively about what's best for the entire Euroland economy. They were so biased about what was going on in their own national economy that they were forced to remove the name of their country from their nameplates when they sat in meetings, in a bid to make them think like 'true Europeans'.

NO:

It is fanciful nonsense to think that we have democratic independent control over our interest rates now – they are largely determined by economic developments in the global economy and by well-tried financial rules. If the European Central Bank raises interest rates, that puts extra pressure on the Bank of England to raise them also.

Nor would it be less democratic in Euroland than it is now. Since the Labour government granted independence to the Bank of England in May 1997, politicians have had no say in UK interest rates. Instead they have been set by a committee of appointed bankers and economists (some of whom aren't even British). Almost all economists agree that – with their technical expertise, ability to think long term and freedom from electoral pressures – central bankers are much better at setting interest rates to ensure stable and low inflation than politicians are.

At the moment, European interest rates take no account of what is happening in the UK, even though they have a big impact on us. If we join, the UK will not only be taken into account, but we will have a vote in what happens to interest rates across all of Europe. In the long run, we will actually have more control over interest rates.

2.2 Will Brussels dictate our taxes?
YES:

The euro project is called EMU, which stands for *Economic* and Monetary Union. Its designers see unifying currencies as only the first step towards unifying taxes, and for very powerful economic reasons. For the euro to work effectively, strong co-ordination between interest rates and how governments tax and spend is required. It will not work if national governments repeatedly undermine the European Central Bank's interest rate policy by altering taxes and changing spending. It will seem as though the ECB is pressing the brake while the national governments are pushing down on their accelerators.

The pressure would not just be on overall levels of tax, but also on the levels of different types of tax, such as income tax and corporation tax. Brussels already sets strict limits on what value added tax (VAT) the government can set, a piece of our sovereignty we surrendered many years ago.

To work effectively, the euro will require a large central budget to even out the adverse effects of the 'one size fits all' interest rate (see 1.1). This central fund – the equivalent of the federal budget in the US – will be needed to make booming regions bail out ailing ones. This large fund can only come from taxpayers.

Having European-style taxes forced on us would seriously threaten our competitiveness. Euroland taxes are a sixth higher than ours overall, and are much higher for businesses. Social security contributions amount to 12 per cent of total labour costs in Britain, compared to 32 per cent in Germany and France, and 28 per cent across Euroland on average. According to the European Commission, tax is just 38.5 per cent of GDP in the UK, far less than the 43.9 per cent average in Euroland.

NO:

British tax levels and the issue of membership of the single currency are completely separate and totally unrelated. Britain retains a veto on tax issues in the Council of Ministers, the highest-level body in Brussels. If Britain doesn't want tax harmonisation, it simply will not happen. Brussels and most of our EU partners tried to force the UK to change our 'withholding tax' on savings, but we resisted and said no.

In any case, there is no need to harmonise taxes – indeed it would be a hindrance. If recession looms in one country, that government can kick-start their economy by cutting taxes or raising public spending of their own accord. This use of our national budget would enable a British government to stabilise our economy throughout the business cycle and counteract any adverse effects of the 'one size fits all' interest rate (see 1.1).

For this reason as well, the single currency does not require a large central budget to operate. There is no need for booming countries to transfer funds to ailing ones – national governments can simply loosen their purse strings to boost their economy. In any case, the Brussels budget is limited to 1.27 per cent of European GDP up to 2006, and can only be increased by a unanimous vote.

YES, BUT:

It is the official policy of both the European Commission and the European Parliament to harmonise taxes. Both institutions have called for each EU country to lose its national veto over tax policy, and the French and German governments support this. This pressure will increase when the EU admits Eastern European countries, making the granting of a veto to every member country increasingly unwieldy.

Gerhardt Schroder, the Chancellor of Germany,

has said: 'The times of individual national efforts regarding employment policies, social and tax policies are definitely over.' Romano Prodi, the President of the European Commission, has said: 'As long as the [veto] on taxes exists, the EU will be like a soldier trying to march with a ball and chain around one leg.'

As well as the political and economic pressure to harmonise taxes, if we join the euro we will be accepting explicit and direct controls on how much the government can tax and spend, as a result of the Stability Pact (see 2.5).

2.3 Will it mean we have to pay the Italians' and Germans' pensions for them?
NO:

This is explicitly banned under the Amsterdam Treaty, which makes clear that no country will be bailed out by the others – they are not liable to pay each other's state pensions in the future or fulfil any of the others' government commitments. In black and white, it declares: 'A member state shall not be liable for or assume the commitments of central governments, regional, local or other political authorities . . . of another member state.'

The Growth and Stability Pact is specifically designed to pre-empt such problems, and get a resolution long before they become an issue.

YES:
That is all very well in theory. The OECD (Organisation for Economic Co-operation and Development) think-tank calculates that unfunded pension liabilities are 139 per cent of GDP in Germany, 113 per cent in Italy, and just 19 per cent for the UK. The House of Commons Social Security Select Committee has concluded: 'The extent of the unfunded pension liabilities in certain of our European partner countries casts serious doubts upon the long term sustainability of their finances.'

In the real world, if the Italian economy, completely burdened with debt, is in danger of collapsing, other European countries will be forced to help out to ensure stability of the European economy as a whole.

NO, BUT:

Such a solution would simply be politically unacceptable in all member states of the EU, who would insist that Italy, say, takes sufficient preventative measures to ensure that it can meet its pension liabilities. In any case, the liabilities are highly sensitive to minor changes in retirement ages and easily controlled.

YES, BUT:

There may not be direct transfers from us to the Italians. But the euro will inevitably lead to a large central budget administered by Brussels (see 2.2). We will have to contribute to that fund, and it would almost certainly be used to bail out those countries that need the money most. One way or another, we will pay.

2.4 Will joining mean we end up with all the red tape that encumbers other failing European economies?

YES:

Levels of regulation in Euroland are far higher than in Britain, giving its countries inflexible economies with inflexible labour markets and high unemployment. In France, it takes £2,105 and six weeks to set up a new business, compared to only £260 and one week in the UK. Alan Greenspan, the revered Chairman of the US Federal Reserve, has said: 'US businesses and workers appear to have benefited more from the recent advances in information technology than their counterparts in Europe. The relatively inflexible, and hence, more costly labour markets of these economies appear to be a significant part of the explanation.'

By tying ourselves more closely to Europe through the euro, we will be tying ourselves more closely to all the extra red tape. Indeed, this is why the TUC in Britain wants to join the euro – it sees a unified currency as a route to getting European-style employment legislation.

NO:

This is a red herring. There is more regulation in mainland Europe, but this is nothing to do with the single currency. Legislation motivated by Europe – such as the working time directive and unpaid paternal leave – has been incorporated into UK law even though we are not in the euro. This has been the result of other agreements we signed up to.

Furthermore, the fact is that European economies are not failing. In France and Germany productivity per hour worked is 20 per cent higher than in Britain, giving them comparatively higher wages. This prosperity is more evenly shared in continental Europe than in the UK, which has extremes of wealth and poverty not seen on the mainland.

There clearly is a problem with regulation, and it is widely recognised in Europe. Otmar Issing, chief economist of the European Central Bank, has said: 'One scientific study after the other, as well as an impressive array of political declarations, not least in the context of European summits, point to the rigidity of European labour markets and the misguided incentives provided by the social security and welfare systems as decisive causes for the continued alarmingly high level of unemployment.'

Some European problems – like high unemployment – have national causes, and the solutions are national. Many countries, such as Spain, have made huge advances in deregulating their labour markets, and for them unemployment has plummeted.

YES, BUT:
There are few signs of reform other than in rhetoric, which we have heard for a decade. Instead Europe has taken many steps backwards, such as France's recent introduction of a 35-hour working week, increasing the inflexibility of already rigid labour laws. Professor Jürgen Donges, head of the committee of economic 'wise men' which advises the German government, has said: 'Global investors are staying away because they don't believe the Europeans have the will to tackle badly needed reforms. The weak euro is a message to each country that they must make fundamental reforms if Europe is to benefit.'

2.5 Wouldn't it mean surrendering our sovereignty?

YES:

Joining the euro would involve a major surrendering of sovereignty, severely hindering our ability to run the economy as we see fit. We would lose control over interest rates (see 2.1), and the ability to manage the economy through taxing and spending (see 2.2). Instead, it would be run by European committees.

If we join the euro, we will be accepting direct and explicit legal constraints on the government's ability to tax and spend. If we were to go into recession, the government would no longer be allowed to spend its way out. Under the rules of the Stability Pact, we would not be allowed to have a budget deficit of more than 3 per cent of GDP, and we would have to keep overall levels of public debt below 60 per cent of GDP. If we broke these rules, we would be subject to massive fines of billions of euros. The government would not even be able to decide its own budget, but would have to submit it to Brussels for prior approval.

Most leading bankers and politicians believe

that, for the euro to do well, most major economic decisions – such as tax and spending – will have to be made centrally, rather than by national governments. The decisions made on setting taxes and public spending priorities are central to any nation state. Parliamentary democracy has depended on the willingness of electorates to be taxed by governments whom they have freely elected. It is not compatible with self-government to hand power over direct taxation to EU institutions. Even Kenneth Clarke, one of the leading campaigners for the euro, admits that Britain's ability to tax is central to its democracy.

NO:

These constraints are there to stop any one country free-riding on the others and make sure each pays its own way. Building up excessive national debts is something that countries should avoid anyway for their own long-term wellbeing.

Within those constraints, countries would be able to tax and spend in whatever way they like. They can pursue high tax and high spending policies or go for low tax and small government. In

France, government spending accounts for more than half of GDP, whereas it is a third in Ireland – and yet both have adopted the euro.

When it comes to interest rates, we would in some ways get more sovereignty. Being represented in the ECB would give us more influence over the business cycle, because we would be there as part of the decision-making process, not just having to accept decisions made by others that would have a profound effect on us.

We will be pooling our sovereignty, not losing it. Compare it to the plight of an individual person. If abandoned on a desert island, you would have total personal sovereignty and could do exactly what you want. But you would still want to surrender that total sovereignty by coming back to civilisation – and all its laws and regulations – because that would be a small price to pay for the benefits of living with and co-operating with others.

In any case, if we don't like it, we can always reassert our sovereignty by pulling out. History has several examples of currency unions that were reasonably smoothly dissolved.

2.6 Doesn't monetary union inevitably lead to political union?

YES:

In Britain, politicians pretend that the euro is just a matter of economics, but in Europe politicians are open about the real agenda: the creation of a single European superstate. Many economists and central bankers say it will be essential if the euro is to succeed.

Wim Duisenberg, the Dutch first President of the European Central Bank, said: 'The process of monetary union goes hand in hand, must go hand in hand, with political integration. EMU is, and was always meant to be, a stepping stone on the way to a united Europe.' Germany's Foreign Minister, Joschka Fischer, said that the single currency was a step in the direction of full political union: 'The introduction of the euro was a profoundly political act. We must put into place the last brick in the building of European integration. There must be a translation from a union of states to a Federation.'

Central bankers warn that the euro can only succeed if there is central control over policies of taxation and spending, and if Euroland isn't made up of nation states all pulling in different directions. The highly respected German Bundesbank issued two formal statements, in 1990 and 1992, saying that monetary union would be durable only if accompanied by political union. Otmar Issing, the Chief Economist to the ECB, has said: 'There is no example in history of a lasting monetary union that was not linked to one state.'

If Britain does give up control of its economy by joining the euro, it would face immense pressure to accept other forms of political integration. Most of our European partners are working towards a single foreign and defence policy for the whole of the EU, and an ever more harmonised justice system. Europe has already taken the first steps to creating a pan-European army with the creation of the European Rapid Response Force.

NO:
Britain has the right to veto any changes to the way Europe is run. The key decision-making body in Europe is the European Council, which

consists of the elected heads of government of each EU country. We can block any changes we don't like.

History also proves that you can have monetary union without political union. The Irish Republic was in a currency union with the UK from 1921 to 1979 without becoming part of the UK. Brussels and Luxembourg had a successful currency union for many years while maintaining separate governments.

Nor do all European politicians want political union. The Dutch European Commissioner Frits Bolkestein has said: 'There will never be a federal centralised European superstate, not now and not in the future. Any thought that the EU might be extended into some sort of superstate is pure fantasy.'

In any case, integration of some sort shouldn't just be seen as a drawback. After a 70-year period when Europe went to war with itself three times, closer integration has ensured no war in western Europe for half a century. It has tied countries closer together economically and politically, helping to end permanently the centuries of animosity that have repeatedly torn the continent apart and cost tens of millions of lives.

2.7 Isn't it part of a plan by the Germans to take over Europe?
YES:
The Germans dominate the euro and its institutions are based on German models. The European Central Bank – responsible for the currency of twelve supposedly sovereign countries – is based in Frankfurt. The Germans are actively trying to make Frankfurt the financial capital of Europe ahead of London (see 3.4).

By forging ahead with integration, the Germans are defining the rules, which are inevitably biased in their favour. For example, the European Central Bank is explicitly based on the German Bundesbank, with the same philosophy, same inflation target, the same method of setting interest rates, and the same lack of openness.

The Germans not only got their own way with the location of the bank, and its constitution, but they even succeeded in defeating France and getting their own favourite candidate, Wim

Duisenberg, as ECB's first President. Based in Germany, a disproportionately large number of ECB staff are German. If we join the euro, our interest rates will be set by a bank that is a German creation.

Many German politicians – and French ones – are explicit in their desire to create a United States of Europe. Germany – the most populated and richest country in Europe – would enjoy by far the most influence and power in such a superstate.

NO:

This is just xenophobic scaremongering. The Germans and French share a similar commitment to bringing greater co-operation in Europe, but Britain retains a veto on any move. Obviously if they push ahead in one area, and we opt out, it will be they who make the rules. For example, the ECB would naturally have had a home in London if we joined the euro, but there is no way it could be in the British capital if Britain stayed out. The only way to make sure we get what we want is to be actively at the heart of Europe, not by acting the club bore, slumped in a chair in the corner, mumbling 'no' to everything the others try to do.

Indeed, further integration is the antidote to excessive German power, rather than the catalyst for it. The French have always been explicit that their real interest in the single currency was to constrain the new strength of Germany after it reunited West and East. Many mainland European countries – invaded by Germany twice last century – think that one of the explicit advantages of the European Union and closer integration is that it inextricably binds Germany to them. Tying Germany and themselves so closely together both economically and politically will make sure that Germany never goes to war again. They see economics as the best preventative for latent German militarism. After all, conquering your customers and suppliers is not good for business.

2.8 Wouldn't staying out mean a loss of influence for Britain?

YES:

The Finance Ministers of countries in Euroland attend informal meetings of the Euro-12 group, from which Britain is excluded. These discussions will be used to develop policy ideas and initiatives that Britain cannot influence at an early stage.

When it comes to European legislation governed by majority voting, Britain will find it difficult to locate allies outside the euro. We will also have less influence with the US, because Britain will be on the fringe of Europe and so less useful. The US has been cultivating a closer relationship to Germany rather than the UK because of its position at the heart of Europe.

Sir Andrew Stark, former British Ambassador to the United Nations, has said: 'It is ludicrous to suggest that Britain's global influence would be enhanced by ruling out the option to join a successful single currency.'

NO:

Staying out of the euro will mean we retain a greater level of sovereignty, and so more influence. By being an independent country, we will clearly be better able to pursue our own agenda and exercise all in our power to achieve that end. As just one more member of the Euroland, we will hardly be worth knowing.

Sir John Coles, former head of the Diplomatic Service, has said: 'Real influence in the world comes from the quality of your assets, the political will to use them, and the skills you bring to bear. We can produce all those and go on using them whilst staying in sterling. I am pretty sure that, on balance, by staying out, we shall gain influence rather than lose it.'

2.9 Wouldn't losing the pound mean losing an important national symbol?

YES:

The pound sterling is a major national symbol for Britain, thought to be the longest continuously serving currency in the world. It has served us well for 1,200 years, through the Middle Ages, through the Empire and through two world wars. It has spent much of its existence being the dominant currency of the global economy.

It is as old as the language we speak, and has become part of it and part of our literature. 'In for a penny, in for a pound' doesn't sound quite the same as 'in for a cent, in for a euro'.

Europe is already trying to make us get rid of

pounds and ounces, and now we are being told we must get rid of pounds and pence. It is all part of the harmonisation imposed from Brussels, and the rubbing out of national differences. The loss of the pound will be a severe blow to British identity and culture.

NO:
The pound has had a long history, but not always a proud one. It has lost more than 96 per cent of its value in the last century as it faltered and floundered and devalued and had to be rescued. Not so long ago the pound was worth more than $5; now it is worth a third of that.

The history of the pound also illustrates its changeable nature. It has spent most of its life as a purely notional currency: the only real units that existed being subdivisions such as groats. Only in 1489 did the pound come into physical existence with the launch of the gold sovereign. When paper currency was introduced in the 19th century, it caused an uproar, with many declaring it immoral. People protested about change when we got rid of shillings and decimalised the currency. History has made fools of both these sets of stick-in-the-muds.

Nor is it a significant part of our identity. If you asked people in the street what it means to be British, they are more likely to say the Queen, democracy, tolerance, a sense of humour, support for the underdog or football than they are the pound coin. It is rather sad to insist that our national identity is so weak that it depends on the coins in our pocket. The French would laugh at such an idea. The pound is just a way of paying for things that is past its sell-by date.

2.10 Would it mean the end of the Queen's head on our banknotes?

YES:

The euro notes, standardised across Euroland, will not have the Queen's head on them. Originally, there was to be a space on the euro notes for a national emblem – such as the Queen's head. But in a typical act of euro harmonisation, this was ditched. They will now have the same design on both sides in every country. If we join the single currency, European bureaucrats and foreign politicians will have succeeded where Hitler failed, in knocking the Queen's head off our notes.

NO:
This is a totally spurious argument that shows a rock-solid ignorance of the history of our banknotes. It is true that the Queen's head would not be on our euro notes – but Hitler could never have achieved this feat for the simple fact that we didn't have the Queen's (or any monarch's) head on the notes until after the Second World War. The Queen's head has only appeared on the notes since 1960, having been made possible by the nationalisation of the Bank of England in 1946. In Scotland and Northern Ireland, where private banks still issue banknotes, the monarch's head has never been on them, and so there will be no change.

In contrast, we have had the monarch's head on our coins since the Middle Ages, and that *will* continue. Countries in Euroland can put a national symbol – such as their monarch – on one side of each coin.

3. What Does it Mean for Business?

Introduction

Britain's businesses are at the front line of the debate about the euro – they will be the most immediately and obviously affected if we join. All the shops, banks and accounts departments in every company will have to switch over. Importers and exporters to Europe will find they are dealing with their customers and suppliers in the same currency rather than a different one. British companies will not be isolated from the changes that the euro will bring to European industry.

Nor will British business remain unaffected if we stay out. Many are concerned that a floating exchange rate and the cost of currency conversion will put them at a competitive disadvantage if we stay outside.

Retailers, exporters, multinationals and small traders all have different interests and concerns about the single currency, and their opinions on the issue are deeply divided. Different business groups such as the Confederation of British Industry, the Institute of Directors, the British

Chambers of Commerce, and the Federation of Small Businesses have all taken different stances and squabbled bitterly over who represents the true voice of business.

3.1 Won't converting to the euro be very expensive for shops and other businesses?

YES:

Cashpoints, tills, and vending machines will all have to be changed or simply bought anew. Accounting systems will have to be switched, and staff will have to be retrained.

The British Retail Consortium estimated that it would cost shops £3.5 billion, and amount to almost 3 per cent of turnover for small shops. Simple price education – producing charts and tables to explain the new prices – will cost around £300 million. The Federation of Small Businesses reckoned that for most of its members, conversion will cost up to £5,000 – a substantial sum for a small company.

Estimates of the total cost vary between 0.5 per cent and 1 per cent of GDP – or up to £10 billion – although the accountants Chantrey Vellacott estimated that the bill for British business would be closer to £36 billion.

NO:

It is a one-off cost that will not be repeated. Much of the cost will just be a case of bringing forward an investment (changing to the next generation cashpoint earlier) rather than a whole new cost.

Costs can also be minimised – possibly as much as halved – by taking measures such as launching during a quiet trading period, and introducing the currency in a 'big bang', rather than letting the two currencies circulate simultaneously.

In any case, much of British business is having to convert its operations to the euro even if Britain stays out (so-called eurocreep). Many exporters are now having to price their goods in euros rather than pounds when they pitch for sales in Euroland. Even companies who don't sell to Europe are having to make an internal switch. Many of the multinationals that operate across Europe are requiring UK suppliers to sell in euros even to their British operations. The Senior Managing Director of Toyota, Yoshio Ishizaka, has said: 'We are now asking our suppliers in the UK to do business with us in euros (instead of pounds) so we can minimise currency risk exposure.' The fact that much of the backbone of British industry is already converted to the euro, will reduce the costs of switching over.

3.2 Will joining the euro make it cheaper to do business across Europe?

YES:

Businesses will no longer have to bear the cost of exchanging currencies as they import and export from Germany, France and Italy. The Confederation of British Industry has estimated that it 'will reduce business transaction costs by 0.4 per cent of GDP'. The European Commission has estimated that the total saving is about 0.33 per cent of total economic output for the whole continent, or a saving of about £20 billion a year. For companies that do business across the continent, the savings are particularly big – one car manufacturer estimated that the euro would cut its costs by around £150 million a year. All these savings will be made year in, year out.

But even bigger than this would be the savings from not having a volatile exchange rate with our biggest trading partner – the EU (see 1.5). A volatile exchange rate makes it very difficult to plan, and if it goes in the wrong direction, it can wipe out profits.

NO:
The majority of British companies would not benefit from this because they simply don't do business with Euroland. Almost eight out of ten small businesses do all their business within a 50-mile radius of their office. Overall, only 15 per cent of all companies do any trade with Euroland, although they would still have to bear the cost of converting to the euro (see 3.1).

In any case, Internet purchasing and electronic money transfer are bringing down the cost of buying using another currency. Overall, savings on transaction costs would be a largely trivial 0.1 per cent of GDP.

To avoid the risk of exchange rate volatility, British companies can buy 'forward contracts', 'hedging' against any adverse movements for up to a year ahead, and ensuring they sell their goods or buy their supplies at a set price in the future. This costs a small amount, but lets them guarantee future profits. Joining the euro would also make us more exposed to volatility against the dollar (see 1.5).

YES, BUT:
They can only insure the sterling value of a known amount of foreign exchange revenue over the next year or so, and it costs them to do it. If they could insure themselves effectively, the strong pound in 1998/9 wouldn't have forced British manufacturing into recession while the rest of Britain was booming.

3.3 Will British businesses be at a big disadvantage if we stay out?
YES:
They will have to face the uncertainties and costs of a volatile exchange rate that has been eliminated by their competitors elsewhere in Euroland. Before the euro, any company outside Germany that wanted to sell into Germany faced an exchange

rate risk, whether it was located in Britain, France or Italy. But today, companies in France and Italy face no exchange rate risk, while those in Britain do.

Companies in Europe are also undergoing a wave of mergers and restructuring in order to arrange their production on a least-cost pan-European basis. This is creating economies of scale previously seen only in the US, of which British-based companies can only dream.

Euroland businesses are also now able to raise money for investment across the entire single currency zone, making it easier and cheaper. British companies, on the other hand, are still largely constrained to drumming up money from within Britain if they want to expand.

The ease of raising capital and the advantageous economies of scale within a single market mean that a successful new company in Euroland will expand far more quickly than the equivalent in the UK, giving Euroland a similar lead in new industries to that of the US. In contrast, British industry faces a currency risk that impedes trade, discourages investment and deters medium-size firms from expanding abroad.

NO:

We are already part of the single market, and getting rid of the barriers put up by having separate currencies will make little difference. It was the removal of all the other barriers – such as tariffs – that mattered far more. The economies of scale are already here – from the EU's almost 300 million consumers – and having an effect. In or out of the euro, British companies can still operate in Europe, and European companies can operate in Britain. Staying out, we have the advantage of a more flexible economy, more adaptable labour market, and lower taxes. All these factors give us an edge over other European countries that we would potentially lose if we surrendered our currency (see 2.4).

If you are unconvinced by the theory, look at reality. Far from floundering, the British economy continued to thrive after the launch of the euro, and two years later it was in the best shape it has been in for a generation (see 1.9).

3.4 Will the City of London lose its position as Europe's financial centre if we stay out?

YES:

The European Central Bank – the second most powerful in the world – had a natural home in London, but ended up in Frankfurt because of our indecision over the euro. This success reinvigorated Germany's bid to ensure that Frankfurt becomes Europe's financial centre, with a massive office-building programme to rival London's Docklands. Both Frankfurt and Paris are very open about trying to stimulate the 'virtuous circle' of success that has taken London to pre-eminence, and their determination would undoubtedly increase if it became clear that Britain's absence from the euro was permanent.

Sir Michael Jenkins, Vice-Chairman of Dresdner Kleinwort Benson, has said most banks still assume that Britain will join when making investment decisions. However, he warned: 'Were this assumption to be put into question, it would lead to a serious rethink by foreign owners of many of the City's financial institutions about where their core activities should be located.'

NO:

This scaremongering – prevalent at the time of the euro's launch – has simply not been borne out by events which show that the launch of the euro has actually consolidated London's number one position. Lord Levene, the Lord Mayor of London at the launch of the euro, used to warn about the threat to London, but the evidence was so overwhelming that he quickly changed tune.

Indeed, London's rivals have suffered a bloody nose because the centralising effect of the single currency means that what were effectively regional financial centres – such as Paris – lost any reason for their existence and saw all European business drain away to Europe's real financial centre, London.

The use of computers and telecommunications means that finance is a footloose industry that technically can operate from just about anywhere. But this works in London's favour – whether or not London is in the eurozone is an irrelevance. What isn't an irrelevance is the fact that London completely dominates financial services in Europe, with a far bigger pool of skilled labour. More people work in financial services in London than live in Frankfurt, its only likely rival. We have the English language and a time zone that means we can deal with New York and Tokyo in the working day.

The City enjoys a self-reinforcing cycle of success – attracting skilled people, capital and liquidity – and this cycle has not been broken by our absence from the euro. Banks have trouble attracting staff to Frankfurt because few people want to live there. The excitement of London – its nightlife, restaurants and culture – means it is easy for banks here to attract the best staff from across Europe and America, who can then do business with Euroland over the phone.

The figures speak for themselves. Before the euro, Paris could claim 4 per cent of the world foreign exchange market, mostly in francs. Now there are no francs, and all that trading has gone to London, which has been able to capitalise on its expertise. Paris not only no longer has a central bank, it no longer has any significant foreign exchange market.

London's share of the euro derivatives market is

94 per cent, almost a monopoly. In 1999, two-thirds of money raised in euro-denominated bonds came through London. In the two years after the launch of the euro, trade in Euroland stocks quadrupled.

Even the Germans are now paying tribute. Rolph Breuer, head of Deutsche Bank and Chairman of the German Stock Exchange, has said: 'London will no doubt remain the leading centre in Europe thanks to its advantage of size, excellently qualified personnel, and the attractive tax, legal and cultural environment.'

Sir Eddie George, the Governor of the Bank of England, put it more bluntly. He simply said it was 'illogical' to claim that the City had suffered.

3.5 Will staying out of the euro put foreign investors off the UK?

YES:

Foreign investors like Britain because it is a gateway to Europe. The report *Business, Britain and Europe* by Anderson Consulting said: 'British success in gaining foreign investment is due to our position as a gateway to the European Single

Market – over two thirds of the exports of the top 20 UK based foreign investors are destined for somewhere else in Europe.'

When every European currency was different, each country carried the same currency risk for foreign investors. Now all the countries in Euroland have no currency risk for investors wanting access to the main market, whereas the UK does. If investors want to avoid exchange rate risk, they will have to avoid the UK.

Foreign investors such as Sony, Toyota and Honda have all made clear that they want Britain to join the euro, as have 80 per cent of German investors according to a report by the German–British Chamber of Commerce. Nissan said it would not produce its new Micra in the UK because of the currency situation. Honda tried to shift all its UK production towards the US market, because it became impossible to compete with producers in Euroland.

NO:
Since the launch of the euro, the amount of inward investment into Britain has risen to record levels.

In 1998, there were 23,300 foreign firms doing business in the UK, but by 2000 this had jumped almost 25 per cent to 28,777, according to Dunn & Bradstreet. In 1998, total inward investment was £204.5 billion, but a year later – after the euro's arrival – it had risen to £252 billion.

Short-term currency fluctuations are simply less important than Britain's long-term competitive advantages of low tax and light regulation, which we can only maintain if we keep control of our economy.

Most of the inward investment comes from US high-tech business, which is pretty insensitive to currency, and comes because of our competitive advantages. It is only a few industries, based on large-scale production for export with small profit margins, that are particularly concerned about whether or not the UK is part of Euroland. However, they get a lot of attention, because these industries, such as Japanese car production and steel, are very high profile.

YES, BUT:
The total inward investment may have grown in

the UK, but it has grown even faster in Euroland. As a result, Britain's share of foreign investment in Europe fell after the launch of the euro. A report by Ernst and Young showed that in 1999, Britain's share of net inward investment projects fell from 28 per cent to 24 per cent of the European total, while France's share rose from 12 per cent to 18 per cent.

4. What Does it Mean for Me Personally?

Introduction

Economic, business and political arguments are all very well, but what will the euro do for me personally? While no one remains immune from the indirect impact of economics and politics, joining it will also have a far more direct impact on everyone. We would, obviously, have to get used to a new currency and new prices. But there are longer-lasting issues surrounding our joining the single currency, such as the impact on mortgages, the prices in shops, and pensions.

4.1 Won't it be confusing changing notes and coins and prices?

YES:

It will be far more confusing than decimalisation, when the prices in pounds stayed the same, and only the pence part of prices changed. Then we kept the same notes, and many of the same coins.

Adopting the euro would mean an entirely new set of prices for everything, and an entirely new set of coins and notes. Consumers would suffer a double whammy of confusion, with the change-over coming shortly after shopkeepers had to change from weighing produce in pounds and ounces, to kilos and grams.

NO:
Any confusion will be reduced by a period of dual pricing – where shops show prices in both currencies – followed by a period of dual circulation, with both coins in use at the same time. This will give customers sufficient time to get used to both the new prices and new coinage.

YES, BUT:
Retailers are pushing for as short a period of dual circulation as possible, because of the cost and complexity of running tills with two currencies. Having two sets of currency in your pocket at the same time is bound to lead to widespread confusion. The old and innumerate will be at the biggest disadvantage.

NO, BUT:

It is a short-term, one-off effect which can be quickly overcome. When people go on holiday, even the most financially illiterate feel at home with a new currency within a few weeks, and it will be the same with the euro.

4.2 Will joining mean cheaper goods?

NO:

When we change from pounds to euros, there will be widespread confusion about prices, giving shops a green light to hike them up. When shops convert their prices from pounds to euros, they will no longer be at convenient 'price points' like 1.99 or 2.99, but at an awkward number in between. It's a safe bet that new prices will be rounded up not down.

Converting to the euro will also cost businesses, and shops in particular, billions of pounds (see 3.1), and that is bound to be passed on to their customers. The euro will also lead to higher inflation and more red tape, encumbering businesses and their customers with even higher costs (see 1.6).

YES:

Most shops will display dual prices in both pounds and euros for more than a year, reducing any confusion, and getting people used to the new prices. We will have both currencies circulating for two months simultaneously, making it even more difficult for shops to hoodwink customers.

In any case, any initial trend towards an upward lift in prices will not continue for long. There will be far more powerful forces – price transparency and economies of scale in a massive single market – that will continuously push the price of British goods down to European levels (see 1.6). The euro will lead to massive savings.

4.3 Will it make it cheaper to go on holiday around Europe?

YES:

Before the creation of the single currency, travellers touring this fragmented continent could spend large amounts of their money simply changing it from one currency to another. The European Commission has calculated that an energetic traveller visiting the other fourteen members of the EU, and changing currency each time, will lose half their money in exchange costs. If they started with £1,000, they would end up with just £500 before having bought a thing. If we join the single currency, these exchange costs will be eliminated.

Joining the euro will also make it cheaper to send money around Europe. Sending money to book a holiday cottage in another country with another currency can cost £40. Within Euroland, it would cost less than one euro – much less than one pound.

NO:

These savings are a mere fraction of the total cost of going on holiday. Normally you only go on holiday to one country and change currency once, adding only around 2 per cent to the bill. On the other hand, costs could rise sharply if we bring the value of the pound down against the euro in order to join at a sustainable exchange rate, reducing its purchasing power in Euroland, and making the whole holiday sharply more expensive.

Britons will find holidays particularly unaffordable if we join the euro and it throws the UK into a semi-permanent recession. To the rising numbers of jobless, the question – of whether the euro makes it cheaper to visit other EU countries – would be academic.

4.4 Will it make my mortgage cheaper?

YES:

Britain has almost always had higher interest rates than Germany, the main Euroland country, and has had higher rates than Euroland since its launch. If we join the euro, it will mean generally lower interest rates and thus lower mortgages. If we had joined at the start, for example, we would have had to halve our interest rates, meaning that the cost of a mortgage would also have halved. If, say, we had to cut interest rates by 2 per cent to join, then that would cut about £80 per month from a standard £50,000 repayment mortgage. This would mean an immediate increase in the standard of living for mortgage borrowers.

NO:

Britain has now put its high inflation, high interest rate past behind it, and the differences in interest rates between Britain and Euroland have recently become more marginal. Indeed, they now have virtually the same long-term interest rates, so getting a long-term fixed-rate mortgage will cost much the same whether or not we join.

In any case, if it did suddenly mean cheaper mortgages – as was the case in Ireland – any benefit would be very quickly wiped out by the resulting surge in house prices. Those who happened to own a house and had a mortgage at the time of joining would benefit at the expense of those who have yet to join the property market (see 4.5).

4.5 Will joining affect house prices?
YES:
Joining the euro would probably mean a one-off surge in house prices, followed by even more volatile prices than we have at the moment. The euro would mean cheaper mortgages (see 4.4), but because that makes buying a house more affordable, house prices will rise. In Ireland, joining the euro led to a rapid doubling of house prices.

The housing market is likely to be far more volatile – and far more dependent on the European Central Bank – than elsewhere in Europe. The UK has far higher levels of mortgage debt than other EU countries, and a far higher proportion of those are on variable rates. In Germany, 90 per cent of mortgages are fixed rate, so homeowners are little affected by rate changes. Britain's housing market is also likely to be more volatile because it has far lower levels of tax on housing than elsewhere in Europe. The tax – or 'stamp duty' – on buying cheaper houses is just 1 per cent of the house price in the UK, compared to 12 per cent in Belgium. That makes buying and selling houses easier – which is good for a flexible economy – but it also makes house prices more sensitive to inappropriate interest rates.

NO:

Joining the euro will have little effect on house prices, and would not make them more volatile.

The independent Bank of England has made great strides to permanently reduce inflation in Britain, bringing long-term interest rates very close to those in Euroland. There will be no one-off boom as there was in Ireland – in effect we managed this all by ourselves in 1998/9 when people got used to low interest rates, which rapidly forced up house prices. Joining the euro would have led to a house price boom if we had joined in 1990, but it will now have no such effect.

Low and stable interest rates have made long-term fixed-rate mortgages very attractive, and more and more Britons are taking them out, reducing the differences in sensitivity to changing interest rates between us and Germany (see 1.3). The Government has also already sharply increased stamp duty – particularly on more expensive houses – bringing it into line with the rest of Europe.

The biggest cause of volatility in house prices is volatile interest rates – as in the early 90s – and joining the euro would generally mean more stable interest rates, and so more stable house prices.

4.6 Will it affect my pension?
YES:

Joining the euro means that we will end up helping the Germans and Italians to pay their pensions, leaving less money for the UK government to pay for our own (see 2.3). Joining will also put severe limits on how much the government can borrow (due to the Stability Pact), further limiting its ability to pay British pensions.

NO:
There is absolutely no connection between the euro and pensions, or the euro and taxes. If there were any Brussels-inspired move affecting pensions (which would be independent of the single currency), the UK government would have the right to veto it.

In any case, if the move were to harmonise pensions, that would be good for British pensioners because European pensions are almost all far higher than ours. Indeed, joining the euro could indirectly enhance British pensions. UK pension funds would be able to get better returns by investing across the entire Euro-area, having the choice of the best opportunities on the continent, not just those in the UK.

5. So, Should we Join?

Introduction

Even the most passionate eurosceptics and europhiles concede that there are strong arguments for and against joining the euro. People tend to want to join the euro for economic arguments, yet want to stay out for political ones. But what matters more: politics or economics? Even within the realm of economics, there are clear benefits and clear costs to both joining and deciding to stay out.

Then there are also the questions of timing, of whether the euro is proving successful, and whether, if we join and don't like it, we could get out. If the euro were to show signs of falling to pieces, it's unlikely the British government would try to take us into Euroland. Shouldn't we just put aside all these academic arguments, wait and see if the euro works for other countries, see how we do outside it, and then decide? Or will that leave us permanently behind Europe?

Many of these answers are a matter of opinion. But, having considered all the issues, the ultimate question you must ask is: do the benefits of joining outweigh the costs?

5.1 Isn't the euro a weak, unstable currency?
YES:

When it was launched, euro-optimists predicted it would rise in value against the dollar. But instead, its value started to plummet. From being worth $1.17 at launch in January 1999, it dropped in value to below $1 before the year was out. City traders dubbed it the 'toilet currency' because it was going down the pan. The European Central Bank publicly insisted it was not concerned, while repeatedly putting up interest rates to try and restore the euro's value.

And yet still it kept on falling, so that before it was two years old, it had fallen below 85 US cents – a loss of almost a third of its value. Its constituent currencies – such as the Deutschmark – were at their lowest level for almost twenty years.

Eventually, there was so much concern that the floundering euro would destabilise the global economy, that central banks around the world – including the Federal Reserve in the US and the

Bank of England – made a historic move, using millions of pounds of public money to buy the failing currency in an attempt to prop up its value. After that, the European Central Bank had to make solo bids to support the euro.

NO:
Global currency swings are by their very nature unpredictable, wild and often uncontrollable – indeed that is the very point of the euro, to stop this sort of thing happening within Europe. The Japanese yen has made similar swings against the dollar, but no one has suggested that *it* is a failing currency.

The weakening of the euro is not a mark of failure, but reflects a mixture of historical, economic, and financial factors. The constituent currencies of the euro – the deutschmark, franc and lira – grew very strong before the launch of the single currency as optimism in its success grew. The subsequent fall in value was simply a case of 'what goes up must come down'.

It is also the case not just that the euro has been weak, but that the dollar has been astoundingly strong, reflecting the unprecedented and pro-longed boom in the US economy. When the boom faltered at the end of 2000, the euro rose against the dollar. Exchange rates have always been highly volatile, and tend to overshoot their fundamental equilibrium value.

5.2 Hasn't the euro failed to live up to its promise?

YES:

The euro was launched in a blaze of europhoria, with huge parties across Europe, and euro balloons released to the sky. Politicians whose mother tongue isn't English made confident pre-dictions that the euro would rival the dollar as the global currency of choice, that oil markets and central banks would all turn to the world's youngest currency. The main problem for the euro, economists said, was that it would grow too strong against other world currencies as everyone tried to buy into it.

But compared to that fantasy euro, the real euro has been a non-stop disaster. Even before its launch, the euro's credibility was damaged by countries fiddling official figures in order to 'show' they were economically fit enough to join. The launch of the European Central Bank was almost derailed, and its credibility severely hit, when France kicked up a huge political storm over the failure of its own candidate to be elected as the Bank's first President.

In the euro's first year, the whole European Commission resigned in a fraud scandal, the Euroland economy performed dismally, Italy broke its treaty promises to reduce government debt, and, as a result, the new President of the European Commission said that Italy might have to drop out. Almost as soon as it was launched, commercial banks were saying the euro had a growing credibility problem. Its value dived as confidence waned, forcing central banks around the world to intervene in order to prop it up (see 5.1). The Danish public defied the united ranks of their politicians, business leaders and media and said in a referendum that they wanted to stay out. Newspapers endlessly speculated about when it would collapse.

The euro not only failed to deliver on its initial

promise, it had just about the worst possible start without actually falling to pieces.

NO:

All the external events – such as the resignation of the Commission – were unfortunate to say the least, but the fact that the euro withstood them shows how robust it is. They are little more than high-profile distractions from the very real advantages that the euro is already bringing.

Even before its launch, the euro proved beneficial for the European economy. In their bids to meet the tough economic entry criteria for the euro, countries such as Italy and Greece, which had always failed to live within their means, finally found the political will to reverse the swelling tide of national debt. This self-discipline is proving very positive for their own economies and for Europe as a whole.

Despite repeated predictions of disaster, the actual launch of the euro was technically perfect. The joiners locked their exchange rates together, creating an unprecedented period of economic stability in Europe. It created a sea of tranquillity in Europe during the Asian financial crisis, which knocked the rest of the world economy from pillar to post.

The euro – and the price stability within Europe that it brought – has already started transforming the competitiveness of Euroland businesses, setting off a wave of restructuring and consolidation as companies take advantage of the vast new single market. Georges Jacobs, the President of the European Federation of Industries, said two years after its launch: 'People now ask "Why did we wait so long to create the euro?" because it makes life so much easier in the single European market.'

The collapse in value of the euro, while politically embarrassing, has actually helped boost the Euroland economy. Exporters drove up their sales by about 30 per cent in the two years after launch, as their goods became cheaper to customers overseas. Overall, economic growth has accelerated, and unemployment in Euroland has fallen.

5.3 Could the euro fall to pieces?
NO:

The euro is a single currency, and there is no way

that currency speculators can gamble against it till it falls apart, as happened earlier with the Exchange Rate Mechanism. You can no more speculate by buying francs and selling marks than you can by buying £5 notes and selling £10 notes.

Nor can a country simply decide to leave. There is no provision in the Maastricht Treaty for a member country to leave the euro. Once a country is in, it is permanent, with no legal exit route. It is an irrevocable joining of currencies.

YES:

Treaties are all very well, but then there is the real world. If a country decides unilaterally to pull out, there is no way the others would send in the tanks. Romano Prodi accepted this political reality when he took up the job of President of the European Commission, and warned his fellow Italians that if they don't do better at controlling inflation, they may have to drop out of the euro.

Countries could have many incentives to leave. By constantly applying the wrong interest rates, the euro could lead to massive unemployment;

one country could get fed up with the financial burden of others repeatedly not living within their means and raking up huge budget deficits. One quite possible scenario involves the electorate of one country getting disillusioned with the euro; an opposition party runs for election on a promise to pull out and wins. There is little other countries could do. One US economist predicted that the euro could lead to such big tensions between countries that it would lead to war before collapsing. Already there are signs in many Euroland countries that people are losing faith in the euro.

NO, BUT:

It would be very costly for countries to leave; they would not do so lightly. Those who predict that the euro will fail are eurosceptics who predicted it would never get off the ground in the first place, and then when it did, that it would be blown apart before launch by speculators. It did get off the ground, it wasn't blown apart, and it won't fall to pieces.

5.4 Isn't it a dangerous experiment?

YES:

Economists cannot accurately predict even simple things with long histories, such as inflation. Trying to predict the consequences of the single currency – the largest, most complex piece of economic engineering ever attempted – is guesswork, however educated. It could turn Europe into an economic superpower, or it could destroy its economy for generations. Belief in one scenario or another is often little more than that: belief. Given the uncertainties, and the costs if we get it wrong, it is simply not worth taking the risk. Sir Eddie George, the Governor of the Bank of England, has said openly that joining the euro is a 'leap of faith'.

NO:

Not joining is also a leap of faith. Being outside a currency that most of the European Union has adopted puts Britain in quite a new situation. Too much of the euro debate is just hankering for an old world in which the euro hadn't been created. The reality is that we are a middle-size country right on the border of a massive and expanding single currency trading block. The superficially 'safer' route of staying outside – until the arguments for joining are beyond dispute – is riskier than joining now.

5.5 Shouldn't we wait and see whether it is successful?

YES:

The euro has had a turbulent start, and it is not clear whether it will succeed, or even last (see 5.1, 5.2). There are many predicting that it will collapse. In the meantime, the British economy is thriving outside Euroland.

While there is so much doubt over the impact of the euro, and its very future, it would be potentially disastrous to join. Joining the euro now could prove as unwise as trying to board the foundering Titanic, insisting you were told she was unsinkable.

It would be far better to wait to see whether the euro works and brings advantages, and for it to gain an established track record of stability, before we even consider joining.

NO:

The euro is a fact of life on the mainland, and it is inevitable that we will join at some point. We should therefore join as soon as possible, to ensure we don't get left behind and are not made to sign up from a position of weakness.

The euro is already making European businesses more competitive, widening the gap with British ones. Foreign investors are already redirecting their investment away from the UK to Euroland. Without being part of Euroland, the rules of the new currency are being set by France and Germany without any regard to British interests.

If we don't join now, we will be in a far weaker position when we finally do. We will make the same mistake we made in joining the Common Market – we waited while the rest of Europe raced ahead until it became more difficult for us to join, and then we scrambled on board at the last moment.

5.6 If we join and don't like it, can we leave?

NO:

There is simply no provision in the Maastricht

Treaty for others to leave, and no provision for the UK to leave. Like all members of Euroland, once we are in, we are in. The decision is irreversible. Romano Prodi, President of the European Commission, has said: 'By definition it's a permanent decision. You cannot enter into monetary union thinking you can do so for five years or so.'

YES:
It is true there is no provision in the Maasticht Treaty for any country to leave, but likewise there is nothing other countries can do to stop you. It will be expensive, but we could simply pull out and set up a separate currency. History has many examples of currency unions that have been successfully dissolved. Ireland, for example, pulled out of the pound sterling, and Russian republics pulled out of the rouble.

5.7 Do the benefits outweigh the costs?
YES:
There are huge economic advantages to joining the euro and huge disadvantages in staying out.

In contrast, any drawbacks are either small, or easily countered.

Having currency stability with our main trading partners will be an immense boost to our economy, far outweighing the drawbacks of having a 'one size fits all' interest rate, which can easily be mitigated against. Any of the short-term costs of joining – such as converting tills – are insignificant compared to the boost that business and trade will get from becoming part of the large single market of Euroland.

If Britain stays out, we will lose out as European industry outstrips us in terms of competitiveness, and foreign investors decide to stay away.

NO:

Any benefits that the euro could bring are small, but the potential costs are huge.

The savings in foreign exchange costs are small, the effects of increased price transparency unknown. The eradication of currency fluctuation within Euroland will bring some advantage, but it will be dwarfed by the economic hazards of being permanently lumbered with wrong interest rates, increased currency instability with the US, more European red tape and a lesser level of sovereignty.

While the euro remains unproven, there is also the very real risk that it could collapse completely, at absolutely colossal economic cost. It will also be unbelievably costly if we try to pull out once we have joined.

With small benefits and big drawbacks, it is simply not worth the risk.

Appendix

Table showing GDPs of countries in the Euro-area, in comparison to UK, USA and Japan.

	Population (in millions)	GDP (£bn)
Austria	8.1	139
Belgium	10.2	165
Finland	5.2	86
France	58.8	956
Germany	82.0	1,406
Greece	10.5	83
Ireland	3.7	61
Italy	57.0	775
Luxembourg	0.4	13
Netherlands	15.7	263
Portugal	10.0	74
Spain	39.4	394
Euro-area **Total**	301.0	4,276
UK	59.2	949
USA	269.1	6,127
Japan	126.5	2,920

All figures taken from 1999 (*Source*: OECD).

Acknowledgements

Thanks to the campaign groups Britain in Europe and Business for Sterling for their excellent pamphlets, which supplied many facts, figures, direct quotes and subtle arguments; Alan Houmann, who lent his expertise; and Paula, who put up with me.